I0796780

CHRIST
THE LIFE

CHRIST THE LIFE

A Gospel Psalm

Thomas L. Martin

PARACLETE PRESS
BREWSTER, MASSACHUSETTS

2022 First Printing

Christ the Life: A Gospel Psalm

ISBN: 978-1-64060-595-4

Readers will recognize in this creative work elements of Scripture across the tradition of English translation. Often, I have "Englished," as it was once called, from the Greek myself. —T. Martin

Cover and frontispiece artwork by J. Kirk Richards. Used with permission.

Library of Congress Control Number: 2020941302

10 9 8 7 6 5 4 3 2 1

Published by Paraclete Press
Brewster, Massachusetts
www.paracletepress.com

Printed in India

The most beautiful poem in the world appeared when God spoke his Word in time. The life of Christ is that poem.

Reader, give breath to my feeble song,
and find your way in his poem.

—T. MARTIN
2022

Contents

The Carpenter

Hands pull a draw knife across the soft grain of wood. Curlicues rise up like white roses and gather at his feet. Tribute to a king? The carpenter blows the dust from the fragrant board.

Adjusting his angle of sight, he regards the shape emerging there. Hands run to and fro across its surface. Study more than eye can see. Light from the window illumines the work. Sawdust glows on fingers like pollen ready for flight.

Knowledge deep in those hands. Care and art. Hands continue to shape. Whorl of fingertip over grain of wood, like galaxies of intent passing over a new creation.

(Matthew 13:55, Romans 8:22, John 1:3, Psalm 96:12)

A Riddle

Two grips. One tight on chisel, one light on mallet. Between left and right hold a riddle. Together tap a code. Neither chisel nor mallet understands.

Mushroomed over, they crouch down, fix their joint focus, and knock heads.

The wood before them yields. If it understands no better, it yields and in yielding somehow trusts. Senses something more in rhythms of lightness and strength. Senses something more under the gathering splinters.

Tapping continues. The lovely form appears not a wedge but a tail. The place it adjoins not a void but its mate.

The two fashioned pieces meet. Hand and hand they grip.

Vertical grain meets horizontal.

The perfect dovetail joint.

(*Ephesians 2:10, 2 Corinthians 1:22, Ephesians 2:22*)

The Service

Near thirty summers lie on those shoulders, nearly wide as the hewn lumber they bear. How many framesteads have they erected, how many rafters raised? The years have brought him to full manhood.

A quiet life he has lived, a life of hard work and peace. Speaks of his heavenly Father whose will he seeks. Finds peace in highest submission. Has any man who ever lived wanted no more, no less?

But then again without ambition, where can life go? No strength can be found in service. Service to father, mother, brother, sister, other is no road to mastery. No beginnings in greatness at the quiet end of a plane and saw.

And yet he carries out his work with joy that astonishes. Every joint fitted, every carving, every new purpose put to wood a revelation.

(*Luke 2:52, Mark 10:45, John 17:13*)

Pursuit of Kings

Kings pursued his life—once.

Kings once to kill him, kings once to kneel to him. One brought sword for slaughter—his brothers, the young hope of his race. Others brought tribute for praise—gifts for a prince, or God, or sacrifice.

Fights over him now over. The adorable little one gone. Babies don't stay they say. Each day they fade till not a trace remains.

When do we become unseemly in our elders' eyes? When do they cease seeing in growing frames endless possibilities? Is he now just Joseph and Mary's boy?

A neighbor passes and thinks what a shame the Life amounts to no more. Hardly old enough to take his place in the temple. Already a has-been. Another possibility forgotten. Another forgotten might-have-been.

All strange beginnings now gone.

Purpose lost in sawdust and forgetfulness of time.

Gone and simply standing before his father and years of houses built, among cupboards prepared, among tables furnished.

(*Matthew 2:7–13, Mark 6:3, Psalm 23:5*)

Shepherds Watch

Shepherd staffs and watchful eyes mind huddled flocks. But for a twitch of a flank or dreamy stamp of a foot, the sheep are quiet now. In the cool of the night, shepherds speak words of calm over their charge. Stand under stars and speak peace. Sing comfort to a congregation that does not understand.

Amid their lyric murmurs, one prophetic word sounds the dark, rolls over wooly back, down hill, across a troubled land. Might Messiah live in our time. Might he lead us. Might he walk among us as a shepherd watching over his sheep.

(*Luke 2:8, Psalm 23:1, Ezekiel 34:11*)

Star Trail

Old riddles, more mysteries. But not to wise men, how many years ago, Daniel's heirs in Babylon.

Magi who read some obscure text in a library of stars. Moved on a sole sign from heaven. Saw the finger of God in a point of light.

Dress in royal finery and gather royal offering. Travel on camel back across desert sands to see the Life.

Seek the consolation of the ages at the end of a star trail.

(*Matthew 2:1–12, Micah 5:2*)

Incarnate

Infant hands reach up. Mary numbers fingers, counts vertebrae, marvels at the miracle of skin.

Tender movements of muscle and bone. Rise and fall of newborn breath over supple limbs.

Auguries and annunciations still seem a dream.

She bundles the Life in his swaddling clothes and ponders in her heart. Thinks how God's heavenly word might be wrapped in human flesh.

(*John 1:1, 14, Luke 1:26–38, 2:6, 19*)

No Room

No room in the inn. Nowhere in this city of man. Never room for God around here.

Nature always first to arrive. Her humble emissaries gather around the scene. Some part of her knows, fills with longing.

Stabled animals mutely share the glory.

Shepherds lay down their staffs, encircle the living creatures.

Ancient wise men as from an hourglass drop into the scene.

Enigmatic gifts they bring of regal gold, divine spice, and burial balm. Set before him wealth from the earth, tears from the flowering libanos, and fragrance from the thorn tree. What does it mean?

All these bend toward a feeding trough in a cow stall in Bethlehem.

(*Luke 2:7–16, Matthew 2:1–11*)

Dedication

The baby held in a column of light. Old Simeon holds the little Life in arms upstretched.

Like Moses holding hands high on a plain in Rephidim. On Nebo's height glimpsing the Promised Land. Simeon has awaited this moment all his life.

Consecrates the child to the Lord. Wrinkled creases water around his eyes. His tremulous voice rises as the prophets of old.

"Lord, let your servant now depart in peace. For I have seen the salvation you prepared before all nations. The light of your revelation for the Gentiles and the glory of your people Israel."

(*Luke 2:22–32, Exodus 17:8–12, Deuteronomy 34:1–3*)

The Shadow

As they turn to leave, a shadow lengthens in the doorway behind them. His mother sees a black X mark the lighted entrance. Its dark crossbeam is in the way. The old man hands her the infant Life. Sees the barred light, regards her face.

“Mother, a sword will pierce your own soul, too.”

And then more bright, “And thoughts of many hearts be revealed.”

(*Luke 2:33–35, 1 John 4:3*)

One in the Wilderness

A rough figure in rocky wilderness. Years later new signs. Is John one more prophet? Or one more than prophet? No royal figure arrayed in soft garment. He wears camel hair wrapped in a leather belt.

Both father and mother in Aaron's line, but he serves not in the temple. For years his home is the wilderness. From a boy he heard the word of God here. Now holds temple in a desert place. Israel empties her cities to hear him.

What has she lost, what does she seek? What draws her to rocky pew and cloudy window? When did her land flowing with milk and honey become a wilderness in judgment? A haunt for wild animals and outpost of foreign soldiers. Glory departed from her streets, dim reminder of the promise. The man feasts on fattened locusts and wild honey. Eats the judgment and the promise.

(*Matthew 11:7–13, Luke 3:1–9, Mark 1:1–6*)

O, Return

His voice cries out, “Return, O Israel. Return to your God.”

A last Elijah at the end of the kingdom. At the end of an age.

“Cleanse yourself for the coming of the Lord,” the Baptizer entreats.

Some new thing he foresees from the dark. A new age beginning.

(*Isaiah 40:3, Malachi 3:1, 4:5, Luke 3:1–9, Matthew 11:7–14*)

Lamb of God

John now on his knees. Before one he announces to the crowds, “Behold the Lamb of God who takes away the sin of the world!”

They know what is a consecrated lamb. They know dedicated to what end. They stand amazed to see the mighty conscience of a nation bow down to him.

John lowered before sandal thongs he says he is unworthy to untie. He solemnly asks, “You come to me to be baptized?”

The man he calls the Lamb answers, “Let it be so.”

(*John 1:29–30, Genesis 22:8, Matthew 3:13–15*)

Baptism

Waters flow over the Life announced. Waters fulfill all righteousness. Bubbling over his eyes, beading in his beard.

He thinks of oil poured over Aaron's head and running down Aaron's beard. Thinks of brothers living together in unity.

The heavens open. The clouds part. Or wings in the clouds? A blinding light.

A voice speaks from above. "This is my beloved Son. In him I am well pleased."

In the light a dove form covers him.

The Life emerges from bright waters. Stands on Jordan's banks. Joshua's threshold. The edge of Promised Land where Yeshua crossed over.

Baptismal waters stream from his robes. The new beginning now.

(*Matthew 3:15–17, John 1:32–34, Joshua 3:5–9, Isaiah 42:1*)

Forty Days

Turn dry lips, drawn belly. Forty days' fast in the wilderness after the voice from heaven spoke. Visceral thunder rolls through his body's void.

Is this the way? Can a man be nourished through his skin or in his breath? But he is sustained by his heavenly Father. Goes without all else to have only him.

He ascends a rocky summit. His wits are whet. Makes his way up the mountain range. Seeks the face of God.

Yes, I hunger in this place where brittle insects march over parched earth. But my soul is fat with the milk and honey of his goodness.

Does someone want to take me away from this feast?

(*Matthew 4:2, Exodus 34:28, Psalm 109:24, Isaiah 55:1–2*)

Apophasis

Announced. Anointed. Messiah.

The voice from heaven clearly spoke: “You are my Son, my beloved Son.”

“Or not,” whispers the Spirit of Doubt.

(*Mark 1:11, Psalm 2:7, Luke 4:1–2, Genesis 3:1*)

Dark in Light

Driven deep into the wilderness. Among careworn rocks on barren ground. Victory and affirmation seem far off now.

After heavenly blessing a test. Why? What good could possibly sprout from desert ground?

Where darkness descends. A shadow falls across the land.

Dragon who would devour infant son returns for the man. But dragon appears not at all. More emperor of the Roman type, or ruler of angels appears in radiant light.

(*Hebrews 5:8, Deuteronomy 8:2, Revelation 12:3–4, John 14:30, 2 Corinthians 11:14*)

Temptations

So the temptations came.

Call bread from the skies, demand God come down, compromise yourself.

And on the temptations came.

Satisfy yourself, prove yourself, take Egypt for your help.

And again.

Take what you will, put God to the test, seize power for yourself.

Every temptation Satan tempted God with, every temptation Satan tempted man with, every temptation man ever tempted God with, he tempted him with that day.

Thrice answers the Life. His word, "It is written." God's manna the Life. Word from heaven spoken. Worship God and serve him alone.

And Psalm quoted by tempter about the one the angels will bear up? What of that? Some puzzle or misstep? Holy or unholy Psalm in mouth of Belial spirit? Psalm speaks of foot by heaven preserved that will crush the serpent's head.

So the Devil left the Life.

And the angels ministered to him.

(*Matthew 4:3–11, Luke 4:3–13, Psalm 91:11–13, Genesis 3:15*)

An Arrest

Word of John's arrest reaches the Life on his return. Some reprisal of revenge for mountain victory?

He withdraws to Galilee.

Herod an easy mark for dark powers. The bloody hands of the Herods not finished their bloodletting yet.

The Life takes up John's message. "Repent, for the kingdom of heaven is at hand."

Begins to teach the people.

Would shepherd Israel in a gorge of wolves.

(*Matthew 4:12, 17, 23–25, Luke 10:3*)

Good News

From Galilee to Capernaum carries the good news of the kingdom.

Heals the sick and brings the light.

And prophet's word fulfills, "The land of Zebulun in the land of Naphtali, Galilee of the Gentiles. The people who sat in the shadow of death have seen a great light."

Brings healing in his touch.

Is the good news himself.

Is himself the light.

(*Matthew 4:13–16, 24, Isaiah 9:1–2, 61:1, John 8:12*)

Nazareth Road

On a dusty road from Nazareth, by all appearances speaking to the air.

Always about his Father's business, such peace.

Always doing his Father's work, such rest.

Glory above him, glory ahead.

Never such a son before.

Drawing from his Father's wealth, accounted poor man.

Cattle on a thousand hills, this loaf of bread.

Omnipotence counted out in five digits.

(*Luke 2:49, Psalm 40:8, 50:10, John 6:38, 14:27*)

Lost Sheep

Let justice roll down like a river. From Dan to Beersheba, might righteousness flow like a mighty watercourse.

He seeks the lost sheep of the house of Israel.

Proclaims release for the captives, freedom for the oppressed.

From scattered lands would call together all the children of God.

(*Amos 5:24, Matthew 10:5–7, 15:24, John 11:52, Romans 15:8, Psalm 102:18–22*)

Clay Jars

Clay jars on a stone walk behind a home in Cana of Galilee. Each one drawn down or empty. Each the girth of a man.

Has the joy abated in the wedding feast?

The wine has run out. Improvident host or unexpected guests?

Christ is at table. Anointed one. Might he bless the feast? So his mother asks.

"Woman," he says, "my time is not yet come."

She to the servants, "Do whatever he asks."

Later he instructs, "Fill the jars with water to the brim."

They do everything he says.

Then he to them, "Now draw and take to the steward."

Something reddens in the cup. A blush before its creator, some new testament? Sign of new life and a new way.

Cheer renewed, the bridegroom receives praise. Steward commends the host blessed this day. Says, "Every man serves the best wine first. After all have drunk, they bring out the worst. You till now have kept the best."

Some will never forget. Will think in later years, Oh, for a taste of that wine.

A divinely blessed wedding feast. Between one at the world's beginning and one at its end.

(John 2:1–11, Genesis 2:22–24, Revelation 19:6–9)

The Twelve

After a night of prayer, the Life calls his twelve disciples. A gathering song begins. To the clatter of coins and fish. Lives called to commitment and sacrifice. Begins a growing chorus of clay and man.

One a compromised tax collector sullied in his labors. Matthew too far down a road he once chose and cannot return. The touch of money still clings to what might be Levi's priestly hands.

A care-worn fisherman too often fished all night long to no avail. Peter trolls the depths of his life for what else he knows not. Room in his heart for some greater catch.

Another who might slight a Nazarene. Nathaniel without guile but without seeming direction, too. Unsure about those outside. Is he yet one more choice to change the world?

And with these, two sons of thunder. James and John who might strike others with heaven's fire, but themselves the better deal. Add to their lot the one-time cynic and poetic doubter. And among their number, the fatal traitor.

The Life calls them, unlikely all. Peter and Andrew, James and John, Philip and Bartholomew, Thomas and Matthew, James son of Alphaeus, Thaddaeus, Simon the Zealot, and Judas Iscariot.

A song of redemption begins that peoples afterward take up and nations sing. Its concord from discord these twelve followers together weave and after them tongues and tribes carry across time. The twelve tribes of his kingdom and new Jerusalem become.

(*Luke 6:12–16, Matthew 9:9, Mark 1:16–18, John 1:43–50, Luke 9:54, Mark 10:35–40*)

Tax Collectors and Sinners

Matthew throws a feast of farewell. A rich banquet as he renounces all to follow the promised one.

He will leave his life of sin to follow in those footsteps. Feels the new freedom. Invites friends to follow. Already has gone down highways and hedges with the good news.

Lays everything before their sight. Matthew's table of custom given for a table of welcome. A table of excise for a table of offering. Breads in baskets, curds in bowls, olives, figs, pomegranates, and dates overflow the board.

Says, "Come and partake. I have found the Life. Come and see." Matthew bids to a sumptuous feast. Where all might be given for the pearl of greatest price. They raise with him cups of cheer.

But not all celebrate. Some come dressed in conspicuous righteous garb flowing from an encumbered legalism. Guardians with moral abacuses clicking on their tongues and heavy scrolls brandishing in their sleeves. Point blame at the Life and those who follow. "Teacher, why do you eat with tax collectors and sinners?"

As the room falls silent, no one breathes. Is the gathering over? Has the change in the world stopped? Must we return to hypocritical servitude and the law that kills? Will our feast not be taken up in the great renewal and making right in the end? Or will it disband like every other human feast and its foretaste of glory fail?

Then returns the Life to these accusers, “It is not the healthy who need a physician, but the sick. You masters of the law, go and learn what this means, ‘I desire mercy, not sacrifice.’ Then know that I came to call sinners and not the righteous.”

The truth sounds out like a bell. Reverberates hope far beyond those walls. Salvation is nigh. Cups raise high. Shouts of cheer he raises again.

(*Matthew 9:9–13, Luke 5:27–32, 14:23*)

The Catch

Peter wrestling with wet and empty nets, wresting what living he can from the fretful sea.

The Life comes on board to teach the swelling multitude who follow from town to town. Will make Peter's boat a platform to deliver God's eternal word. Surrounding the boat they follow in the water. He asks Peter to push out from shore and sits down to teach.

"To what shall I compare the kingdom of heaven?" he begins his sermon of similitudes. "It is like a mustard seed that from a grain grows the spreading tree. It is like leaven that breathes life into the bread. It is like treasure in a field a man gives all he owns to have."

"Again, to what shall I compare the kingdom of heaven?" he says. "It is like a mighty net that draws from the sea fish of every kind." Finishing, he turns to Peter, "Cast your net in the deep for a catch."

Incredulous Peter, "Master, we have toiled all night and caught nothing." In the space of a quiet gasp think Andrew, James, and John, "Peter, watch your tongue."

Peter surprises the crew. Trusts beyond his tired sense. "But because you ask, Master, I will do this thing."

Again they lower their nets. This time withdraw a haul so great no man before dared dream were possible. They strain their faith and their nets.

The dripping ropes, flapping fish, and scales on scales shiver the lines. They start to break. The catch overflows two boats that nearly sink in the deep berth.

The fishermen look at one another. What happened here? Fear strikes them to the core. They see a throng in the boat and a throng on land.

"Fear not," says the Life. "From now on, you will catch men."

(*Mark 3:7–9, Matthew 13:31–33, Luke 5:1–10*)

Benefaciendo

The Life goes about doing good. His touch heals the sick. The leper cleansed. The lame walk. The deaf hear. The blind receive sight. Miracles not seen since the founding of the world. Days the Life reclaims from the realm of Death. Miracles of creation made new.

The religious leaders, punctilious keepers of traditions, misread the Scriptures. Uphold customs made by men. Hide extortion under religious robes. Mask hatred behind a hypocrite's frown. Clean the outside of the cup but hold within a posset of dead men's bones.

They say the Life is bastard, foreign-born, demon-possessed. Call him madman and Beelzebub. They are sons of those who killed the prophets, those who read death and bondage in the Word. They seek honor from one another, who read the Lord of the Flies in the Lord of Life.

"If I do not the works of my Father," he says to them, "then do not believe me."

He adds, "But if I do his works, know that the kingdom of God has come to you. Know that my Father has sent me. Know that I and the Father are one."

(*Acts 10:38, Matthew 11:2–5, 23:1–36, Isaiah 35:5–6, Mark 3:22–30, John 9:32, 10:22–38*)

Touchstone

A tale of hearts. Religious leaders outraged raise stones to kill him. Peter abased falls as stone before him. A tale of righteousness and sin.

With obdurate hate in closed fist they would destroy him who brings healing. Brings healing in his wings. Down to the fringes of his garments brings life.

The other figure alone face down in the dust. Sees himself in the presence of God. "Away from me, Lord, for I am a sinful man."

The Life, touchstone of hearts.

(*John 8:48–59, 10:31, 2:24, Luke 5:8–10*)

The Keepers of Tradition

He walks through unseen hedges of tradition. He doesn't notice, or perhaps he does, how these customs of men mark spaces to go and not. Regions of life and death.

He passes through what is left in a world of rock breakers. Those remains in the dust by many masters. Too many masters in Jerusalem.

What is left of Moses' freedom, of Elijah's heavenly fire?

What else but rules and rulers. Hard laws and cold hearts.

Rocks held high over the heads of religious leaders. Raise their hands against the Life. They will have submission or death.

Death to the Life.

(*Mark 3:1–6, John 8:44, Leviticus 26:11–13, 1 Kings 18:24*)

Fisher in the Dust

But Peter is prone in the dust of death.

Opens his hands. Stays for an answer. Seeks the cure.

"Peter, you choose not the way of the others?"

"Where can I go, Lord?" says the weathered fisher, lying in the dust. "You have the words of eternal life."

His rough heart seeks grace. Lifted by the rough hand from the stony path.

"You shall be the rock, Peter."

A hewn rock and chosen foundation. When one stone will not be left on another, he will be fixed in the temple of God.

(*John 6:67–69, Matthew 16:18, Mark 13:2, Ephesians 2:20, Revelation 21:14*)

Sermon on the Mount

Moses ascended the mount alone to receive the law. One like unto Moses takes the people with him.

The Life goes higher. Writes God's law on their hearts.

Adultery, murder, greed begin inside. Empty yourself of hate, drain away vainglory, forsake all pride. Weep for your poverty of spirit. Hunger and thirst for God. Seek with all your might. He will fill you if you ask with all your heart.

He comes not to change one jot or tittle of holy law. Shows what the law has said all along. Is himself the divine fulfillment.

Blessed the higher way he proclaims. Blessed are the poor and the meek. Blessed the pure and the gentle. Blessed those who seek mercy and peace. Blessed those who suffer for righteousness' sake.

No law for the powerful. Not for grasping hand or mastering mouth.

Bless in return for hate men give you. Overcome evil with good. Bless those who hurt and despise you.

What a world this would be if all followed his word. A world he starts now. His new rule. The kingdom within.

But how? Requires new life. Innocent blood.

Moses descended the mount alone with broken tablets of law. This one returns with his flock and with talk of his body broken.

(*Matthew 5–7, Luke 6:20–49, Mark 8:31*)

The Crop

Fingers rustle through bowing grain stalks. The Life and his disciples pass through a corn field. Golden stalks ripen in the sun.

The disciples rub the grain in their hands. For the hungry followers, a handful harvest. A humble meal thankfully had along the way. As they listen to the Lord, they glean all they can, take in his every word.

Out of the field spring up bearded sentinels of right and wrong. Pharisees who say if a man drags a stick on the Sabbath, he ploughs as he walks. If he drops a seed on the way, he plants. And if he heals the sick with a holy hand, he breaks divine law.

"Teacher, rebuke your disciples for working on the Sabbath!" Their eyes watch his every move. They follow only to find fault. Find what they seek in violation of their rules. Rules upon rules to make their ascent. Rules to control the outsides and not the hearts of men. Rules to stir up pride that swells the dough and arrogates the spirit before God. Rules that wrest the Almighty Lord to human debt.

"Have you never read?" the Life asks them. "When David was in need, and pursued by his enemies, he ate the bread of the presence in the temple of God? And he gave his followers to eat?"

They answer not.

Grain moves with the wind. Wind blows whithersoever it wills.

"The Sabbath was made for man and not man for the Sabbath," he says.

A provision for rest and not a burden to bear. A blessing and not a curse.

His hand waves over the living field like a sacred text. Says, "The Son of Man is also Lord of the Sabbath."

Tares part from the corn as he passes, chaff and grain divide. The disciples follow deeper in the field, partake. The Pharisees, plotting, depart.

(*Matthew 12:1–8, Mark 2:23–28, 1 Samuel 21:3–6,*
John 3:8, Matthew 13:24–30)

The Opening

A sliding of tiles, bits of rubble and dust scatter to the ground in a crowded house in Capernaum. A shaft of light strikes the floor and stays.

Its circle widens. Above the teacher's head appear five pleading faces.

Down they lower their friend on ropes and a cot. His place of confinement far too long.

Bewildered gasps, bemused whispers, all around.

Eyes look to the Life for his response. The littered man now laid before him.

"Son," says the Life, "your sins are forgiven."

More gasps. This time from angered keepers of the law. "Who can forgive sins but God alone?"

But keepers who keep not to their question. Nor see proof in answer given.

"That you may know the Son of Man has power to forgive sins on earth," the Life says, "Get up, take your sickbed, and walk."

The man stands healed with soundness of limb restored. He takes up his cot and walks home, praising God.

Voices amazed drown out the naysayers that day. Will there come a time when his miracles are commonplace? Will there be a time when opinion turns? On this occasion the people rejoice and give glory to God. Say, "We have seen remarkable things today."

(*Mark 2:1–12, Luke 5:17–26*)

The Children

Children laughing in Judea beyond the Jordan. Wide eyes and ready faith, they joy in being with the Life. Some deep connection between these fresh from his creation. Not yet conducted into the world of men.

Their laughs cut off with officious "No's" by those who control those who cannot oppose. Presumed heads of a new order more important as they maintain the claim of who will be the greatest. They miss the lead of the Lord, his soft countenance for little ones he blesses.

Great leaders have no time for children and childish ways. Administrative adults busy in a world of bartering, wagging tongues, and eating the next meal. Blind by the exigencies of what they choose to see. Blind to the future before them. Blind to the past they lost.

Blind to the Life teaching through the children. Teaching we are not the rulers. Not the rule enforcers. Not the judges we think we are. Nor the executioners.

Blind to the now. Teaching us to see again with eyes of wonder and trust. Teaching us not to miss his joy and peace. "Unless you become as a little child," he says, "you cannot enter his kingdom."

Lest we forget, the Life teaches through the children.

Teaches the many ways we are not God.

(*Mark 10:13–16, Matthew 19:13–15, 18:4*)

Centurion

The foreigner's faith in Capernaum. A Roman centurion.

The captor's heart captive by the holy rites of a humbled nation. Yet in its present state sees something more powerful than in the most powerful empire the world has known. Enough of the former glory remains here for a seeker of what is real. He partakes of the holy observance. Knows salvation is of the Jews. Out of his devotion builds them a tabernacle.

Sends an emissary of the nation's elders to the Life, "Lord, I am not worthy for you to come under my roof. Say but a word, and my servant will be healed. For I am a man under authority, and, as I speak, those in my charge come and go. So I did not presume to come to you."

Astonished at the man's faith, the Life says, "I've not seen such faith. No, not in all Israel."

In that same hour was the centurion's servant healed.

(*Matthew 8:5–13, Luke 7:1–10*)

Come Home

Small man takes height from a tree. Seeks material for a higher prospect.

Wants to know what the massing crowds mean.

This Zacchaeus paved his own way with others' coin. Ill-gotten gain, he is traitor to his race. One foot in mother Israel and one foot upraised with Roman power.

He never could put gold under his feet. Sought heaven in a foreign face stamped in metal luster.

Outcast. Mistrusted. Zacchaeus standing in neither camp.

Wealth and power he desired and desired got. But cost him all too dear. Too much soul given on the open market. Ringing coin in currency he can no longer afford. In his hands lie the flat gods on flat worlds.

The Life looks at him and says, "Zacchaeus, come down. I am visiting your house today."

The Master knows his name. Time to go home, Zacchaeus. Time to return.

"I will return, Lord," Zacchaeus says. "All I have defrauded others I will return fourfold."

"And give half my possessions to the poor."

Zacchaeus, time to come home.

(*Luke 19:1–10*)

The Touch

Twelve years and all her money on doctors gone. The woman's issue of blood will not be staunched. No, not after all the vain attempts and failed assurances from physicians who are supposed to know.

And so she suffers in silence alone. No measure of cloth bindings cover a wound that will not heal. No amount of cleansing stops her life draining, sanguining her clothes. "Unclean," the whispers say about her. If the elders know, they will drive her out.

But she sees the hem of the Life's garments. Fixes her eyes past the train of followers to the very edge of his robes. If she could but press through the throng. "If I could touch the fringe of his cloak. If I could get close, I know I will be healed."

And so she extends her hand. Reaches out. A finger touch lifts the curse. Stops the flow. In one touch, she is healed by God.

The Life knows. In that moment, he turns around. In the press of the crowd, he says, "Who touched me?"

The disciples, incredulous in the clamor, "The people push on all sides and you ask, 'Who touched me?'"

"Someone did touch me," says the Life. "For I perceive power left me."

The woman falls before him. Abashed now that all eyes fix on her. Trembling, tells her story.

The Life lifts her up. "Daughter, your faith has made you well. Go your way in peace."

(*Mark 5:24–34, Luke 8:40–48*)

Monuments

Caesarea Philippi, the meeting place of gods and kings. Monument named for its Roman Julius and Macedonian conquerors. Brought justice and peace and hope? Little justice or peace for peoples under their footfall. Just two more chapters in the failed kingdoms of this world. No sign left except the dying echo of a name.

Slits cut in the scarred mountain side, a human assault on the ultimate. Small impressions in rock appear, tiny alcoves where human hands erect pagan deities. There is Hermes, the messenger god sent from heaven. There is Pan, the all and the shepherd god. Monuments both to unknown deity carved on the mountain face, a cabinet of pagan gods.

Worshipers stone-faced behold their idle pantheon. Does hope spring here or religion die? In this place water flows from the rock. Not from its snowy top in rivulets, but a mighty cataract from its side. Its natural landmark says something more. A rich symbol undivined by mind that worships man or four-footed beast. Prays to lifeless stones of earth shaped by human hands. Desperate artisans and resisting granite gods both are breathless in the end. Meanwhile, mighty waters flow from the mountain's side. Life-giving waters where tropical trees and plants rare in desert lands raise a witness to the cleft in the rock.

The Life and his disciples stand facing the towering landmark and voluminous waters. Lost worshipers there, effusive symbols, and dark characters in a Gentile text.

(*Mark 8:27, Matthew 16:13, Acts 17:23*)

Who Am I?

“Who do the people say that I am?” asks the Life.

“Some say you are the prophet Jeremiah,” they answer. “Some say Elijah. Some John the Baptist.”

“But who do you say that I am?”

Peter says, “You are the Messiah, the Son of the living God.”

“Blessed are you Simon, son of Jonah.

“Flesh and blood has not revealed this to you. My Father in heaven gave you this light.”

(*Mark 8:27–30, Matthew 16:13–17*)

Stumbling Block

He explains to them, “Messiah must suffer at the hands of the elders, the chief priests, and wicked men. They will try him and kill him. But on the third day the Father will raise him from the dead.”

Peter speaks, “This will not happen, Lord! I will not let it happen.” Peter assumes mastery. Rebukes his Lord. “Put it far from your mind.”

“Get behind me, Satan!” the Lord turns to Peter. “You do not savor the things of God but the things of man.”

Temptations continue from unexpected places. So quick to go from right to wrong.

Indulgent love becomes an offense, the rock a stumbling block.

“If anyone wishes to come after me,” admonishes the Life, “he must deny himself and take up his cross.”

Does any of us yet grasp what he says?

“Do you really want to follow me?” he asks again. “Are you willing to give all? Then know that those who seek their life will lose it. They who forsake it will find it. Are the ladens of this world greater than the weight of your soul?”

The glory awaits. Carry your cross. Seek the Life.

Up and down the roads with him. Still we do not understand.

The trust comes first. Later the sight.

Says the Life, "Some here will not taste death before they see the kingdom of God come with power."

(*Mark 8:31–38, 9:1, Matthew 16:21–28*)

Transfiguration

Six days later, the Life takes Peter, James, and John with him up a mountain peak.

As he lifts his voice in prayer, his face turns bright. Light shines through his clothes, his countenance like the noonday sun. Is himself the light.

The veil of his flesh in that moment cannot hold, cannot contain the divine majesty. The Son of God shines through the Son of Man. Messiah come in his glory.

Out of the blazing light appear two men. Moses and Elijah talk with him of his death. Of his exodus from this world. Of his glorious ascent. The kingdom come with law and oracle, rule and word. His perfect obedience of divine sacrifice. The gulf bridged, kingdom glimpsed.

Peter from his slumbers struck with fear says, "Master, let us build three tabernacles. One for you, one for Moses, and one for Elijah."

Would you build three shrines, Peter? Would you make permanent this place? What ways have you learned? Forget you again the sacrifice? Forget the promise of the law and prophets? Would you stay the Father's hand? Peter knows not what he said.

A thick cloud rolls down and envelops them. From its midst speaks the divine voice, "This is my beloved Son. He is the one I delight in. Listen to him."

Disciples alone with the Word. His countenance returns, garments no more lightning white. "Be not afraid," he says as he descends the mount.

Turns to them as he walks down, "Come and follow me."

(*Mark 9:2–8, Matthew 17:1–8*)

Come Forth

In Bethany, talk turns to whispers. Little subtlety when looking in the face of death.

Nothing more to do here. Ceremonies concluded, Lazarus' body consigned to dust. Four days past and the spirit gone.

"Why did his friend not come?" speak the murmurs. "He healed the sick. Now the one he loved is dead."

Late arrival and no apology from the Life.

Tears wring the gathered crowd. Too much faith in him? His new way started—life and healing and—and this. Turmoil-stirred faces. Wild confusion at the loss. At the undeniable stone-stoppered tomb.

Faith shipwrecked on a rocky grave.

Martha goes to meet him. Mary the missing one now. "Lord, had you been here, my brother would not have died."

Looking at him, the slightest alteration in her voice. Hazards her faith in the improbable hour, "Even so, I know whatever you ask, God will give you."

She calls for Mary tarrying, who falling at his feet repeats the suppliant accusation, "Lord, had you been here, my brother would not be dead."

Waves of emotion too great to walk on. The Life steeped in grief.

Jesus weeps.

Weeps for friends. Weeps for humanity.

"Look at his love," says one.

“Could he not have prevented this death?” says another.

He guides those gathered to remove the stone.

Martha falters. “It is too late. His body decays.”

Stone between them and the work of God. “Did I not say if you have faith, you will see?”

Men scuff a few hands in their doubtful act. Roll back the resisting rock. What had he said?

It is cold behind the stone.

Silence.

The place of the dead.

He lifts his eyes, “Father, I know you hear me. I speak to you so they may know.”

Too hard for them to believe before stony realities. The place where bones go to bleach.

His spirit groans deep.

Can these stones live?

The Life shouts. His authority breaks the silence. Fills the grave with his word: “Lazarus, come forth!”

Another silence and then a stir of wrappings.

Up rises Lazarus’ body sheathed in shroud.

“Unbind him,” says the Life.

Undam their joys, gasp their exultations.

Cocooned in his grave clothes, Lazarus trails a linen strip. Death unravels before their eyes. His kingdom banner trailing in the dust.

They rush to help. Remove Lazarus' bands like a prisoner set free.

(*John 11:1–44*)

The Laugh

What had he said to Martha?

“I am the Resurrection and the Life.”

She tells the truth to all she can.

And, “He who believes in me though he dies shall live.”

She speaks his word again, “He who lives in me will never die.”

Triumphantly speaks abroad, “That is what he said.” And, “If he had not said ‘Lazarus’ when he shouted, the gates of death would have come down.”

Tells how word of this wonder travels to the religious leaders. How tale-bearers would improve their lot with them. Leaders of what, she wonders, but does not say. Learns they would kill the Life. Learns they would kill Lazarus, too.

Lazarus with her tells the story. He is the living proof.

Some in town warn him to be silent and keep his life.

Lazarus’ eyes flash. Lazarus laughs out loud.

(*John 11:45–53*)

Jerusalem Road

On a dusty road from Bethany again.

Always about his Father's business, such peace.

Always doing his Father's work, such rest.

Glory above him, glory ahead.

Never such a son before.

Returns once more to Jerusalem.

Goes to certain death.

(*Luke 9:51, Isaiah 50:7*)

Occupation

Armored greaves over Roman sandals marching up and down the Judean countryside. Helmets and shields flash in the sun. Might some emperor's warhorse at any moment arrive?

Too many want the heart of your treasure, O Jerusalem. Your God-given wealth you owe to your Salvation alone. Jerusalem, enthralled in the world, forgot her God.

Many pass in and out of her streets, where she keeps a semblance of her feasts. Does she yet know what she wants? More Jerusalem in the hearts of faraway pilgrims. Only a glimmer of glory left inside city walls. Some dim or dying recognition of the glory still to come. How can the latter glory be greater than the former glory of this house?

(*Luke 3:1, Haggai 2:3–9*)

The Ride

Word covers Judea that the prophet of Nazareth has raised Lazarus from death. Blind Bartimaeus and others restored to health. Hopes rekindle for some visitation or deliverance.

Pilgrims stream across the countryside for holy week. Catch sight of massing crowds around one on the way. Hear the cries of rising excitement. Hurry over to see. Can this be the one of whom they speak?

But is this the procession of a king? The Life rides a donkey to the city.

Here no pomp or glory. He rides in slow gait on a colt. Upon which never a man sat, the humble creature shows no signs of bearing the maker of the stars on its back. Walks with undisturbed contentment and inborn duty. Does it bear the Son of David promised to God's people across the ages?

Some disbelieve.

Others recall Zechariah's prophetic words, "Rejoice, O daughter of Zion. Your king of righteousness comes to you in triumph and victory, comes in righteousness and salvation. He is poor and humble, riding on a donkey's foal."

They take off their robes. Bow before him who makes his way to the holy city. Cover Roman roads with Israel's coats of many colors.

(*Mark 11:1–10, Matthew 21:1–8, Zechariah 9:9*)

Hosanna

Salute the Life on all sides with palm branches. Shout, "Hosanna! Blessed is the coming kingdom of our father David. Hosanna in the highest!"

Make an avenue in their gathering green, a mile of waving banners, a thoroughway of praise.

With cries of acclaim, "O save us!" Follow him into the city.

Jerusalem, do you still know what brings you peace? Ariel, are you still the lion of God? Once the spiritual heart, now but the Judean capital. Her urban dwellers and religious officials look askance at such devotion.

Some dressed as leaders crosscut through the crowds. Appalled, exclaim aloud, "Teacher, rebuke your disciples!"

The Life turns to them, "I tell you if they keep silent, the stones will cry out."

(*Mark 11:9–11, Matthew 21:9–11, 15–16, Psalm 8:2, Luke 19:28–40*)

The Entry

Religious functionaries in uniformed officialdom confront the multitude. Leaders followed by numbers of their own forbidding followers. Do their best to douse the flare of religious fires.

Will the crowd's devotion last? How many messiahs in their heads? What will they be shouting a week from now?

The Life walks weeping up temple steps.

(*Luke 19:41–44*)

Let Judgment Begin

The children have long been told of their pilgrimage to Jerusalem. Stand expectant in the temple court, the place where all nations are meant to pray. But where are the supplicants bent-kneed, where the worshipers from all lands? Where the trumpets of welcome from priests in white robes, their call to worship under the burnt offering's smoke, mingled with incense rising to heaven, pulsing to chanted Psalms?

They find instead the crush of a market, barkers and hawkers selling costly wares to those now penned inside temple walls. Listen to endless wranglings over price, hear groans of pilgrims fleeced of their last cents.

Above the confusion in the bazaar rises one clarion voice. A voice of conviction and outrage. A fiery voice of judgment. The Life turns over tables and drives the sellers out. Raises a scourge of cords to cleanse the temple of God. His voice high over the rest, "It is written, 'My house shall be a house of prayer for all nations.' But you have made it a den of thieves!"

Coin stacks and unjust scales clatter to the ground. Their ring lost in the din and the dust. Shrinking moneychangers scrabble on bended knee after the tossed mammon. They, the running livestock set free, and the sellers scatter. In a pillar of cloud and settling debris stands the Life in the temple court as judge.

In that moment, his disciples remember it is written, "Zeal for your house has consumed me."

(*Psalm 122, Mark 11:15–17, Isaiah 56:7, John 2:13–17*)

Authority

"Tell us by what authority you do these things!" demand those obviously in control, judging by their bearing and the outward signs they wear. They pass under the shadow of the Roman Praetorium and Herod's palace to make their way to him. Approach but not close, they huddle together in fear of people who enfold the Good Shepherd in droves.

If these leaders are to get to him, they must find another way.

"Tear down this temple," the Life answers, "and in three days I will raise it up."

(*Mark 11:27–28, Matthew 21:23–24, John 2:18–22*)

Signs

The Pharisees make their own petition, "Teacher, we would see a sign."

He answers them, "In the evening, you see the sky is red and know the next day will be sun. In the morning, you see the louring crimson and know there will be storm. How can you read the weather and not the signs of the times?

"A wicked and adulterous generation seeks a sign. I tell you the truth, no sign will be given this generation but the sign of Jonah."

He says as they prepare to devour him and put him in the ground.

(*Matthew 12:38–40, 16:1–4, Luke 11:29–30*)

Temple

Turning to the high edifice his disciples say, “What lovely stones.”

The temple destroyed and raised again, a towering symbol of his resurrection no one yet understands. An emblem of the Life no grave can hold.

Ezra’s temple raised once more. Solomon’s temple built on rock. At the site of Abraham’s sacrifice on Moriah Mount.

One greater than the temple is here.

(*Matthew 24:1–2, Ezra 6:13–22, 1 Kings 6:1–13, 8:62–66,
2 Chronicles 3:1, Genesis 22:2, Matthew 12:6*)

The Blind

The blind and the lame seek him for healing. Man blind from birth before him now.

The Life works spittle in the mud. Applies it to unseeing eyes.

A hemisphere in shadow, the man has groped all his days in perpetual night. Waiting for the coming of God near a pool that means "Sent." Waiting at the temple for the call.

Moist sand like a shore touching a land long dead. Brings new life to a dark world.

"I don't know how he did it," exclaims the man. "All I know is that I was blind and now I see!"

Has sought with all his heart and found.

Says the hand that made the mud, "As long as I am in this world, I am its light."

Many hands upraised, the testimony of silent hosannas. Fresh signs for those who would see.

(*John 9:1–41, 1:4*)

Adulteress

Stones again in fists held high. A circle forms around one cowering figure.

All fingers point to her. The adulteress. One stoneless hand reaches down. One finger points to sand.

Why? Many hands wave in noisy accusation, one finger stirs in quiet contemplation.

Stirs the stones ground small, split apart and worn down. So reduced the whole world. But among its calcite divisions the divine finger stirs, inside their infinitesimal logic moves. How their games of pulverized legalities would turn her to dust now. Turn him to dust. Give them a few more bits on a path they might trod. Stand firm on this one or two. Bring them closer to God.

Brother for brother, the ground cries out. Cain's mark left on the broken earth in every part.

The same finger that first etched law on Moses' tablets now stirs the stones. That engraved the holy law to draw a freed people to their God. Law broken before his finger formed the last character of the final word.

And what does the finger write in shattered stones? Compose what in a quarry of dust? What impression leave his constellary swirls? Will the message this time hold?

Does he write the law again in sand? Does he write out their sins? Does he write a new command? Or some mystery beyond the grasp of stone-filled hands?

Where is the adulterer? No one appears to know. Written word in sand unnoticed, too. But the fresh-breathed word—some higher law?—of honest grace he speaks. Speaks in living flesh. This word moves.

“Let the one who is without sin,” he says, “be first to cast a stone.”

For just a moment, men see themselves in the glass of his word, see the stones in their guilty hands. Where are the adulterers now? Deep in their pit, the word over their heads resounds.

Men walk out. Stones fall to the ground. Holy word a daybreak of light. Stones the size of a human heart.

He says to the woman, “Go and sin no more.”

(*John 8:2–11, Genesis 4:10, Exodus 31:18, 34:1, James 1:23*)

Preparation

The Week of Preparation. Pharisees, Herodians, Sadducees come in waves to question him.

Rival factions vie over who is the pure and true. Who is closest to God. Who is most chosen.

Enemies reconciled for a day. Must disgrace the one who calls himself God's Son. Must win back the crowds. Must silence the Christ.

Must shame the Life with their greater learning: he cannot stand in the seat of Moses, take David's mighty scepter, speak as oracle of Solomon. As we do.

Adversarial rulers of the nation's soul greet the Life with their unctuous words of praise. Like baited temptations they return anew. "Teacher, we know how honest you are and that you teach the way of God in truth." Adoring tongues lay a net at his feet.

(*Mark 12:13, 18, Luke 23:12, John 7:15, Matthew 22:15–16*)

Image

Pharisees and Herodians first pose a question. Pharisees, exceptional sect, set apart to the law of God. Herodians, whole-souled crowd, sworn to Herod's kingdom of this world.

"Is it lawful to pay taxes to Caesar or not?" they ask. Double-pincer question. On either side condemnation or death.

"Why do you hypocrites put me to the test?" asks the Life. "Bring me a denarius."

"Whose image is on the coin?"

"Caesar's."

"Then render to Caesar the things that are Caesar's and to God the things that are God's."

Questions cease. Tongues grow silent. Divine amazement minted on their faces.

(*Luke 20:19–26*)

God of the Living

The Sadducees would next take hold of his words. They whose dialectical scaffolding long ago buried the ark and forgot the glory and testament inside. Climbed inferential rungs of disbelief to their enlightenment. Israel's long-accustomed rulers too worldly-wise to believe in heaven's world to come.

"Teacher, Moses said if a man dies childless, his brother should marry his widow and raise up a family. Let us say he, too, dies, as do others, up to the seventh brother. Tell us, in the resurrection, who will be her husband?"

A definitive argument for their sect. Turn a law to protect the childless widow to faith in nothing. No one in Zion can answer.

Responds the Life, "You understand neither the Scripture nor the power of God. For those who rise from the dead neither marry nor are given in marriage, but are like the angels in heaven.

"And you say the dead do not rise, but have you not read in Moses how God spoke in the burning bush? He said, 'I am the God of Abraham, Isaac, and Jacob.' He is not the God of the dead, but of the living. For they are all alive to him. You are greatly mistaken."

From that time, they dared ask him no more questions.

Again their mouth traps fail. Recoil on the adversaries' heads. Reduced to silence in the great assembly. Only one way open to them now.

(*Mark 12:18–27, Luke 20:27–40, Matthew 22:46*)

Upper Room

From Bethany one last time the Life directs his disciples. “Go into the city and talk to a man carrying a water pitcher.”

Go to Jerusalem. The only place where the Passover is to be killed and eaten.

“This man will guide you to an upper room.”

Go to Jerusalem. The place I have longed to gather to myself with outstretched hands.

“Go and prepare the Passover meal for us.”

Go to Jerusalem. For it cannot be that a prophet die outside of Jerusalem.

(*Mark 14:12–16, Matthew 23:37, Luke 13:33*)

The Servant

He invites the disciples to his meal.

Wraps the towel around his waist. Sets the basin at their feet. And himself beside.

"Lord, do you wash my feet?" Peter asks.

"What I do now you do not understand."

"Lord, you will never wash my feet."

"If I do not wash your feet, you have no part in me."

Peter accedes, then overtries, on his steps to faith.

The Life puts in Peter's foot. Lifts another dripping foot out. Someone thinks of the baptisms they performed all across Israel. Unclear if Peter thinks of the hand that pulled him from the churning waters.

The Life dries him with the clean linen that covers him. Pink and olive skin blossoms from the towel. Sets the bright flesh on the cool terra cotta.

So he does with all his disciples. Seats them at his table.

"I have earnestly desired to eat this Passover with you."

So welcomes the Lamb.

(John 13:1–17, 4:1–2, Matthew 14:28–31, Luke 22:15)

The Bread

He raises the Passover loaf.

Scorch marks from the oven like stripes across its back.

"This is my body."

He rends it in half.

"Broken for you."

His hand passes the torn pieces. It is warm in their hands.

Incarnate Word the bread? This bread? Physical in spiritual, spiritual in physical. Do they yet understand?

Every word that proceeds from the mouth of God was their bread.

Manna rained down in the desert was their bread.

The one who now extends this loaf once said, "I am the bread."

How can these things be? One at the table remembers that hand passing the loaf to five thousand. Another remembers. And another. Bread for all.

A loaf for the whole world. Bolted, blistered, and broken. Torn into a thousand pieces and a manifold thousand more. Bread enough to feed all the starving race.

Bread to feed hungry souls. Bread that refused divine miracle to feed himself. Bread that fulfilled all the Father's holy commands. Bread that came to serve, not be served. Bread that gave his life for many. The unleavened bread.

The bread of presence. The showbread. The bread of the face of God.

Bread in pieces passed around the Passover table. Bread sent abroad. Bread multiplied around the world.

(Exodus 23:15, Mark 14:22, Matthew 26:26, Luke 22:19, 1 Corinthians 10:16, John 6:31–35, 1–14, Deuteronomy 8:3, Matthew 4:4, 20:28, Exodus 25:30)

The Wine

Likewise he raises the cup. The Passover cup.

From Abraham's son spared to Israel's children freed from Pharaoh's hand.

The paschal lamb raises the cup.

"This cup is the new covenant."

In his blood.

The chastened grape, fruit of the sun, crushed in the cup.

Cup of his blood.

From Ruth's morsel dipped in the wine to the promised days when the hills themselves will drip with wine.

"Drink all of you."

Drink the life in the cup.

"Poured out for you."

Drink.

He passes the cup to his followers.

Foam bubbles on the brim, breathes new life, swells like grapes, gleams like globes in the wine.

"So proclaim my death until I come."

The cup to hushed lips.

"When I will drink the fruit of the vine anew with you in the kingdom of God."

Drink.

Eyes brighten.

A feast forever.

The cup comes full circle.

A last red of sunset washes through the doorway and over the doorposts.

(*Mark 14:23–25, Matthew 26:27–29, Genesis 22:13, Exodus 6:1, Ruth 2:14, Amos 9:13, 1 Corinthians 11:25–26, Exodus 12:21–23*)

The Betrayer

"One of you will betray me," says the Life as he dips a sop in the bitter herbs.

How can this be? Did he not choose each one of us? Have we not followed for three years?

What turns are there in a man's heart? Paths to turn aright, paths to turn away?

What whisper from the dark would turn against the Life? What black thought conceive such evil? What bad faith bring that evil to light? What cold enter a soul to surrender the Life to his foes? Who would cast him down to raise himself up?

What is in my heart? Which way does it bend? I fear its weak graspings and doubts.

Each one of us asks, "Is it I?"

(*Mark 14:17–21, Exodus 12:8*)

The Garden

After the meal, the Life and his disciples make their way, singing a hymn. Settle for the evening in a garden where the olives grow.

The Life sits next to a knotted trunk, under one long, twisted branch.

"You will all abandon me tonight," he says to them. "Pray with me that you fall not into temptation."

What has the ancient tree above them seen, standing almost two thousand years above the Kedron, overlooking the city below? What was that city once? What has it become where the olives grow to ripeness?

"You will all fall away because of me," he says. "Watch with me this night and pray."

A great grief overcomes his soul. Casts him down on his face. "Oh, my Father, if it is possible, let this cup pass from me. But nevertheless, not what I will, but your will be done."

His disciples have gone to sleep. "I am grieved to the point of death," he tells them. "Can you not stay awake with me and pray?"

He prays again in the still night air, "Father, all things are possible with you. Take away this cup. No, not what I will, but what you will." He prays on the ground where the olives are harvested.

His disciples fall asleep once more. "Can you not watch and pray with me one hour?" he asks again.

Alone in his grief. He steps away to pray. They sleep again.

The stars are cold. He lifts his gaze to pray once more. The shadow of the tree looms dark over him. The agony has begun. His sweat falls as drops of blood.

He stands. "Do you still sleep?" he asks his disciples a last time. "It is enough. The hour has come. The Son of Man is delivered into the hands of sinners. Behold the one who betrays me."

He says outside Jerusalem at an oil press called Gethsemane.

(*Matthew 26:30–31, 36–46, Luke 22:44*)

The Price

Judas alone stands before the Sanhedrin. Falls behind the others on some pretense of provision. Taste of bitter herbs lingers on his lips.

"What will you give me if I deliver him to you?" Vast his voice sounds in the mighty hall.

All the reasons expressed and unexpressed why what he does is best.

A hearty agreement between them is struck. The transaction quickly done. The temple officers dole out the price of a man's soul.

Thirty silver coins they count from the holy coffers. What preferment more will come. Thirty silver coins ring in some bright future. What weight the sum presses in his hand.

Judas drops the payment in his purse. The dark inside swallows the cold deposit. The once follower cinches closed the bag. Swings the drawstring from the end of a finger. The hanging ransom of a rich man.

(*Matthew 26:14–16, Zechariah 11:13*)

The Kiss

Flickering torchlight in the dead of night. A small garrison of armed guards comes into sight like a walking watchfire.

Looks more like a mob uprising than a deputation of temple guards. Guards for what, who leave the temple exposed? Armed for what, where the Life prays in a sleepy grove?

Faces appear in the flames. At the head, Judas' smiling face. Is here for one thing only. Stands in a new way. How many lies put that smile on Judas' face?

"Peace, master!" he says approaching and gives him a kiss.

"Judas," says the Life, "do you betray the Son of Man with a kiss?"

Disciples stirred from their slumbers stumble out of sleep, "Lord, shall we smite with the sword?" One strikes the high priest's servant. The steel glances off his head and severs the ear.

"Enough!" says the Life to the bloody outbreak. Touches the gaping wound, makes the man whole.

"Do you come after me as a robber with swords and clubs?" says the Life to the fiery multitude. "When I was with you each day in the temple, you laid no hand on me.

"But this is your hour and the power of darkness."

They erupt again to bind him tightly and carry him off.

Saved, the disciples scatter in the night.

(*Luke 22:6, 37, 47–53*)

Dark Trial

The makeshift garrison clanging arrives at a hasty meeting of chief priests, elders, and scribes.

An unlawful meeting of the Sanhedrin seeks witnesses in the dark of the third hour. Tongues freighted down with cash, giddy with favors, will testify against the Life.

One swears, "I heard him say, 'I can destroy the temple and rebuild it in three days.'" Another, "He said, 'I will tear down this temple made with hands and build another without hands.'"

The high priest turns toward the accused, "Have you no answer before these who testify against you?"

The Life holds his peace. What answer can be given this illicit court?

Caiaphas in the high place exclaims, "I charge you by the living God, tell us whether you are the Messiah, the Son of God!"

"It is as you say," speaks the Life. "And you will see the Son of Man sitting at the right hand of the Almighty and coming on the clouds of glory."

Daniel's visionary word and David's messianic psalm bounce off stiff necks and drown in boisterous outcries. One head above the rest lifts its peremptory voice, "What need we more witnesses? You have heard the blasphemy."

"He deserves death!" they all together shout.

Caiaphas grabs his robes and rips thread after thread in a long histrionic tear.

Before the day is over, a greater hand will tear a more sacred cloth in his temple from top to bottom.

(*Matthew 26:57–66, Mark 14:53–64, Daniel 7:13–14, Psalm 110, Matthew 27:51, Mark 15:3*)

Temple Guards

What joy the temple guards get from giving pain. How arrant their give and take. They rain blows upon his head. Tear the beard from his chin. What pleasure in their sadist's game.

Yet they cannot stand when he looks at them. His eyes must be covered. Avert his eyes. Blindfold the Life.

Tie, too, his hands. They want no striking back.

Then comes the spitting, the berating, the blaspheming.

Shout at him the profanest things heard in this world or the next.

(*Matthew 26:67–68, Luke 22:63–65*)

Judgment Seat

In the fourth hour, the chief priests bring the Life to Pilate.

Ceremonial prayer shawls cover their heads as they stop before Roman halls. Needlework in gold with stitching of white on black. They will not defile themselves in the pagan residence. Drag behind them the bloody man, beaten and bound.

Demand Pilate come to the judgment seat.

"Why, what evil has he done?" asks the governor.

"We would not have brought him to you were he not a malefactor."

"Take him and judge him by your own law," answers Pilate.

One wipes the corner of his mouth, "It is not lawful for us to kill a man."

(*John 18:28–32*)

What Is Truth?

Fire in brass lavers lights Pilate's marble hall. The Life bound fast led inside. Accusations hurled at his back.

"See how many charges they bring against you?" Pilate asks.

The hammered breastplate with its heavy skin clasps imperial before the homespun robes.

"Do you not answer? Do you not know I have the power to free you?"

The governor amazed he answers not a single charge.

"Are you King of the Jews?"

At this the battered and bound Life speaks, "My kingdom is not of this world."

"So you are a king!"

"You rightly say I am a king. For this reason was I born…"

Pilate looks outside at the multitude.

"For this cause came I into the world…"

Pilate on the threshold remembers the dream, his wife's troubled night, "Have nothing to do with that righteous man."

"To witness to the truth."

Stepping into the light, Pilate wryly asks, "What is truth?"

Over his head, Rome's side-glancing eagle. On the other side, the Life. Before them, lion mouths would devour him now.

(*John 18:33–38, Matthew 27:19, Psalm 22:13*)

Scourge

Pilate delivers the Life to be scourged before the people.

The beating of the Roman soldiers alone might kill him. They strike him with the lash, the reed, the fist.

The flagrum's tongues strike in a blinding fury. The cracks burst the air. Rend the exposed skin.

The scorpion ends hunt nerves in the flesh.

The scourging continues merciless.

Not a soft heart in the crowd unshivered.

(John 19:1)

Robe and Scepter

The mocking robe the soldiers give him adorns his flesh now rent.
The purple soaks through patches scarlet red.

And the snarl of thorns they place upon his head.

On their knees with vile gestures they revile him. A rising ovation they deliver with hardened fist. Up and down their waves of abhorrent adoration.

They present him the bullrush scepter. Crashing now on his head. A verge of violence christens the Christ. Drives thorns deep into his brow. In his hand they place the bleeding reed broken. Ceremoniously grant the king his authoritative straw.

After this what could they have planned?

(*John 19:2–3*)

Ecce Homo

"*Ecce homo*," announces Pilate to the crowd.

The Life's visage marred past that of a man. His cheeks swollen, beard plucked, visage torn. The image of God smashed beyond likeness of a man.

The monster we made of the man.

The monster that must die.

(*John 19:5, Isaiah 50:5–6, 52:14*)

Exchange

At the feast on this holy day, Pilate has a custom to release a prisoner to the people.

He stands above them in the Praetorium with a question: "Do you want me to release to you the King of the Jews?"

The priests and scribes had delivered him for envy, he knew. What would *vox populi* say?

They cry out, "Not this man, but Barabbas!" The prisoner Barabbas captured in the insurrection. The notorious murderer and thief.

Pilate has Barabbas brought to stand in the square next to the Life. His dragging chains settle on the pavement stones.

The governor asks again, "Whom will you have me release, Jesus Barabbas or Jesus King of the Jews?"

Jesus Barabbas, son of the father—or Jesus, Son of the Father?

The question hangs in the air. Which Jesus? Side by side they stand. One deliverer from the hills and one from we know not where. One deliverer with a sword and one with the truth. Whom will they choose?

Again the rising wave of voices, "Give us Barabbas!"

Pilate cannot believe. The echo of his wife's voice for the innocent pleads. A sole voice for the Life. Dies in the tumult.

"Then what do you want me to do with your king?"

"Crucify him!"

"But what evil has he done?"

"Crucify him!" again they shout.

Pilate calls for a brass laver from his chamber. On a sea of opinion, he washes his hands before the mob. Then hands over the Life.

The high priest presents the bleeding sacrifice at the judgment seat.

The Roman guard leads him to be crucified.

And Barabbas condemned to die walks free.

(*Matthew 27:15–26, Luke 23:13–25, John 18:39–40, 19:4–6*)

Carry the Cross

The Life commanded to carry his cross. Penultimate indignity for the condemned man. The hand that made the wood to flourish in the world now made to carry the instrument of his death. The holy back Moses prayed to see pass by now cut to shreds and bowed below the unyielding rood.

Driven outside the camp. Bearing his reproach. Climbs his last hill. The stair to his death.

To the sound of scorns and cries he struggles up. The cross nods above his perishing feet. Scraping behind him the weighted beam leaves a line in the earth.

His strength is near its end. He buckles under the load a bloody heap. What he has suffered already? Who will carry the cross with him? Simon of Cyrene steps forward. Another Isaac to convey the wood for ritual sacrifice?

But no escape for the Life. No royal mile for him. From the valley of death to Calvary's dolorous mount. He goes the way of suffering.

(*Luke 23:26–27, John 1:3, Exodus 33:22–23, Hebrews 13:13, Genesis 22:6, John 19:17*)

Nails

The cross at his feet. Heavy in the dust.

What tree since the tree of knowledge gave the wood? Was it the ladened sycamore burdened with fruit? Was it the scented cedar a young carpenter once quartered in boards? Was it the towering cypress brought low for a funeral? Was it the storied dogwood said never again to grow true?

What crude hand hewed the timber that would crucify the Lord? What smithy's furnace in what ore of earth forged the nails? Who lays the Lord of life on this tree of death?

A calloused Roman hand drives the nails through his flesh.

(*Deuteronomy 21:23, Psalm 22:16, John 19:18*)

Golgotha

Into Golgotha's toothless socket, the heavy cross drops in the ground.

Flesh and earth reverberate.

Bulls of Bashan compass him about. Menace their horns of power. Open mouths would raven him now.

The Life in the land of death. Stripped naked for shame. Nailed to the accursed tree. Its fruit swollen in bloody torment.

What unEden is this in late hour?

What last outpost in the city of man?

What last stand of sin?

Surrounded by armies of darkness.

Outside the walls in the place of reproach.

(*Mark 15:22, Psalm 22:12–13, Luke 22:53, Hebrews 13:12*)

Crown

Around his crown of thorns all hell swirling. A blizzard of fiery enmity. The shouting, the spitting, the taunting.

The violent halo they've given him. Behind the human roar, hell's unholy holiday. They win. Will rule. God's plan thwarted.

The Life, proclaimed Son, all but gone. Dark in a penumbra of demonic hate.

(*Matthew 27:29, Mark 15:29–32, Luke 4:13, Ephesians 6:12*)

Go Back

What is the Lord of Life doing on a cross? No sense in a world gone mad. The holy teacher of righteousness. The only one to walk its straight and narrow road. No one deserves death less than he.

Now the world all gone in a rage. Loves darkness instead of light. Shouts with wicked laughter at the Life. Who does he think he is? What does he know, who said he was sent from God?

What good do they find in his agony? What good is their mockery? What good the vicious scoffing to them?

Do they not like the way to God he showed? Not love his tender reproach and call to return? Is there no healing for this fractious world, no balm in a world of poisonous spite?

They believe they are right in the end. The Life causes trouble for Jew and Gentile alike. Let him be gone. Let us go back to the way we were. To buying land, marrying a wife, burying the dead.

(John 1:10–11, 8:46, 3:19, Jeremiah 23:5, 33:16, 1 Peter 2:22, Luke 14:18, 20, 9:59–60)

Serpent Lifted Up

And so will he be. No more. So send him off.

This man writhing in pain. Suffering in silence. Who makes no complaint while cruelty ignites every sinew. The curse floods every vein. He returns not their scorn. Gives not hate for hate.

Whose work is this? How could it come to pass? Whose master plan? What perverse concert of hell and men could conspire to such an act?

Writhing in pain and lifted on a tree. Is he Moses' serpent lifted up?

So he said.

How can one proclaimed the Lamb become the serpent?

What last outbreak of evil could make him the image of sin?

How can one so exalted be so trodden down?

Is the Son of glory that monument in brass? God's anointed this horror in blood?

(*John 3:14, Numbers 21:8–9, Isaiah 53, John 1:29, Psalm 22:6*)

King of the Jews

He speaks.

On the cross the Life speaks.

Under the sign he speaks, disputed by the priests.

JESUS OF NAZARETH, KING OF THE JEWS

What do signs really say to this world? Does it matter after today?

Over the men he speaks, who find more worth in his clothes than in the man. Divide his garments among them. Cast lots for his tunic, unending story of the weaver's beam, one thread from top to bottom. Apparel without seam.

Sign to them of what? A happy prize and windfall of war, wager of nothing more? Tenantless raiment slumped over one soldier's arm as another giddy soldier throws the lots.

Next to the Life shouts a crucified thief, "If you are the King of the Jews," joins the crowd's maniacal cries, "come down from your cross and save us all."

The thief on his other side asks, "Have you no fear of God? We suffer justly while this man did nothing wrong. Jesus, remember me when you come into your kingdom."

The Life says to him, "I tell you the truth, this day you will be with me in Paradise."

The Life numbered with the transgressors.

He speaks on the cross: "Father forgive them, for they know not what they do."

He says with bleeding arms outstretched.

(*John 19:18–24, Luke 23:32–43, 22:37, Isaiah 53:12*)

Sacrifice

Nearby at the temple, the holy smell of sacrifice. The righteous demands of a holy God. Over the mercy seat extended hands.

Up on Mount Calvary, darkness descends. From the sixth to the ninth hour, impenetrable black veils the sun.

Into the chill air, the Life cries, "*Eloi, Eloi, lama sabachthani?*"

Some think he calls Elijah to save him. As we do at Passover's end. They mistake everything he said. To the last word.

"*My God, my God, why have you forsaken me?*" echoes his voice.

He holds fast to the God who afflicts him.

In the deepest ebb of dark the Life declares, "It is finished."

All on the altar now.

With his last breath, "Father, into your hands I commit my spirit."

The Lamb of God slain.

Women who followed him stand at a distance. Crowds behind the soldiers, the mockers, beat their breasts.

His head falls. The Life is gone.

Earth quakes. Rocks break. The curtain in the temple tears in two.

The centurion at his post struck with fear declares, "Surely, this was the Son of God!"

(*Leviticus 16:14, Matthew 27:45–50, Job 13:15, Luke 23:44–46, 48, Matthew 27:55–56, 51–54*)

In Death

The Life in death. Take him down from the bloody timbers. Felled to give life its end. To bring death to a man. Trees cut to lay the Life low.

They rush, as if to make a difference, to lift from the earth the sacred freight. His body in their arms limp. Feet that carried the good news stopped. Hands that healed the sick stilled. All the Life spilled. Face forlorn. Took all that heavenly wrath and earthly hate could give.

Nearby a fresh-cut tomb. One hundred pounds of aloe in stolid stone jars. The Arimathean this day will bury a king.

The holy vestments of the Life all that is left. Joseph holds the body up. In trembling devotion and tears, he drapes the Life across his back.

Himself appears a new cross. A robe of righteousness.

Carries the Life to his deathbed.

(*John 19:38–42*)

Blood Seeds

Blood seeds dropped in the earth. The scorching ground took the savage planting.

More blood—earth the endless sink of human cruelty.

This time is different. Nature groaned to her deepest depths. Sky stays dark and earth still tremors at the Lord now dead.

Now he is buried. Will it be night forever and never again light? Is this the end?

(*Genesis 4:10, Romans 8:22, Luke 23:45, Matthew 27:51*)

Burial

This time is different. Life is in the blood.

The executionary soldier thrust the spear in his side. Out flowed a rush of water and blood.

Water from the rock. Strike the rock of God.

The sent one's blood.

Said it would be this way. We didn't see. Didn't want to believe.

A burial is not a planting, is it? Water a dead earth? Sow dead seeds in a dead land? Death breeds death is the way of the world.

Would that this time were different. Would that this time were eternal blood. Would the water flood the temple and blood transfuse the world.

As we steal away, the earth takes in the water and the blood. Thinks in mineral mind about sacrifice. Ponders it for three days.

(*John 19:33–34, 1 Corinthians 10:4, Ezekiel 47:1–12, 1 John 2:2*)

Sunday Morning

The sun Easters on a blinding horizon.

The interment stone lies flat on its face. The broken monument to Dagon before the ark of God? Just the first pagan monument to fall.

No ark in view, but angels in radiant dress stand guard and point the way.

Say, "Why do you seek the living among the dead?"

An open-mouthed tomb.

Death aghast at the risen Life.

(*Isaiah 60:1–3, Matthew 28:2–4, Luke 24:1–7, Acts 2:24, 1 Corinthians 15:26*)

Risen

After the Sabbath, the faithful women approach to anoint the body. To say a last goodbye, still crying. They watched him die. The disciples nowhere to be seen, still terrified.

No sign, too, of the burial guards whom authorities set to watch. Who will help us? Who will roll away the stone?

Aside, Mary Magdalene weeping carries to the grave jars of aloe and spice.

Sees the sepulchral seal broken. Fears some dire evil has come to violate his lifeless form. Have they not done enough?

Stoops into the tomb. On the cold stone sees the cast-off burial clothes. Sees the blood soaked through.

Does their evil have no end? With her tears anoints his grave anew.

Two on either side unseen ask her, "Woman, why do you weep?"

Mary still does not see. Sees not these two in bright array.

Her heart a tomb. "They have taken my Lord away," she sobs, "and I know not where they laid him."

She will do what she can. If only to cover his death with herbs and perfumes.

She turns away. Before her another figure she thinks is the gardener. Her downcast face a grief of doom.

This one outside the tomb asks, "Woman, why do you cry? Whom do you seek?"

"Sir, if you have moved his body, tell me where."

The risen Life says to her, "Mary."

"Teacher!" she says, stepping from the sepulcher. Tears of joy set free.

"Do not hold on to me," says the Life. "For I have not yet ascended to my Father. Go to my brothers. Tell them I am ascending to my Father and your Father, my God and your God."

She runs to them. Cries in triumph, "He is risen!"

(*John 20:11–18*)

Doubt

Thomas' doubt a gaping chasm. Why choose me? Why did I follow?

I said, "Why don't we go with him so we too can die?"

And now we have gone with him. And now he is dead.

And now we have fallen away. And yet we live.

The shepherd struck. The sheep fled. It all happened as he said.

Still Thomas doubts. Hardly less than Peter's denial. Than Judas' betrayal.

Thomas' doubt, a cloud, ever darkens his life. The void grows about his head, his heart. Never can step from the shadow of his own gallows. Something final this time in his eye.

A follower of one he thought had the answers.

In three years little sun shone through the dark. Doubt as winding sheet wrapped tight. Admit no light, doubter. The Life has died. More reason not to believe. Death is the end of life. Better to believe in nothing.

A man cannot live once he is dead. A Roman death sentence with a Jewish exclamation is the end. My heart from this time forward is a sealed grave.

All figured out. And yet—

(*Mark 16:11, John 20:24–25, 11:16, Matthew 26:31, Luke 22:57, Ecclesiastes 9:3–5, James 1:6*)

Believe

And now they say he lives?

Or just their women's tale.

Hopes, such as they are, dashed. As they are, and ever shall be. A wry end to the last three years.

Dead is known. Dead is done. Dead is finished.

I will not believe. I will not.

One stands behind him. One he does not regard.

One who has been here all along.

"Thomas," he calls. "Put your hand in my side."

I turn to look.

"Touch the breach the spear has made. Touch the void in my hands."

I reach to touch.

Doubt concentrates on three black spots. A triple tear that spilled his Life. The chasm left on his form. Wounds received in the house of his friends.

In his grip the Life holds the darkness, around the void the Life. The dark of the abyss concentrated in his wounds, the evil of the world in his healing hands.

I touch. The doubter sees. Clouds release.

I fall to my knees.

Worship.

Believe.

"My Lord and my God."

(*John 20:26–31, 19:30, Zechariah 13:6, John 11:25, Colossians 3:4*)

About Paraclete Press

PARACLETE PRESS is the publishing arm of the Cape Cod Benedictine community, the Community of Jesus. Presenting a full expression of Christian belief and practice, we reflect the ecumenical charism of the Community and its dedication to sacred music, the fine arts, and the written word.

Learn more about us at our website:

www.paracletepress.com

or phone us toll-free at 1.800.451.5006

You may also be interested in...

Fair Jesus

The Gospels According to Italian Painters 1300–1650

Robert Kiely

ISBN 978-1-64060-258-8
Hardcover | 288 pp | $39.99

"This is a book about how Italian artists of the late Middle Ages and Renaissance interpreted the life, teachings, and miracles of Jesus in their paintings—how they *saw* Jesus."

Robert Kiely goes through major sections of the Gospels, pausing with the Italian painters to consider Jesus, how he looks, how he stands or sits, how he interacts with other figures and the viewer, how his actions and teachings are interpreted and translated by artists into forms without words. Though the book is seasoned with comments by theologians and references to poetry and music, painters and their paintings are the guides to Kiely's text—beguiling, challenging, consoling, instructing—displaying their colors, skill, and perspective while beckoning the viewer back to Scripture and to the Jesus "who accepted to be seen."

"Beautifully written and wonderfully illustrated, this book brings new insights into all that has gone into portrayals of Jesus. It will enhance the understanding of Italian religious art in the late Middle Ages and Renaissance for readers and viewers alike."
—**Sissela Bok**, Author of *Exploring Happiness: From Aristotle to Brain Science*

Available at bookstores
Paraclete Press | 1-800-451-5006
www.paracletepress.com